GW00806371

SCAREcrows

Jon Stone

Happen*Stance*

Acknowledgements:
'Jake Root' was commended in the National Poetry Competition
2009; 'Voronoff's Patient' was first published in *Under the Radar;*
'Malignants' appeared in the ezine *Hand + Star;* 'Bedhair' was
published online in *Horizon Review,* while 'Bullshit-related Injuries'
appeared in the online journal *Poemeleon.*

Printed by The Dolphin Press
www.dolphinpress.co.uk

Published in 2010 by Happen*Stance*
21 Hatton Green, Glenrothes, Fife KY7 4SD
nell@happenstancepress.com
www.happenstancepress.com

Orders:
Individual pamphlets £4.00 (includes UK P&P).
Please make cheques payable to Happen*Stance* or order
through PayPal in the website shop.

Contents ✳

for k

Grand Augur

A bird has shat on your bonnet. Your dinner will burn.

Jake Root

Sure as I'm dying, I need it. Bring
them nuggets of zingiber, fire-packed rhizomes
to mash into candy or jam between pillows—
banish hag-rodeo! Bring that curio
brings me luck, most outrageous medicine,
puts charge in me, want for that juiciest medicine.
Let me gnaw it and gob in the westerly
(right up my back as I'm making the dead run).
Mix it with nutmeg and ground John the Conqueror
so that I might have the upper hand. Bake its
pulp in a bread to gag dapper gamblers
like Death. It's the best bet—ask Dr Bronner
or Dioscorides. Get me that jake root,
that stick of mouth-gelignite, brute tongue-number,
that flashover powder, that head unblocker,
that knothole of daggers, that good thrumming petrol,
that woodknuckle jump-lead, that sting-in-a-knock,
fresh from the citadels, fresh from the spade,
or not fresh—vintaged in mother's cupboards,
stowed in a clay jar, fossilised, strung on
a necklace worn by a princess or priestess
fresh from a grave at the foot of the Andes
or fresh from a boat from the faraway islands
or dangle it still strung from her gleaming neck,
or have her chew it to glistening, hating me.
Whole or in pieces, tenderised, tampered with,
stuck on a blade, in a bowl—but I need it
now and I need it now and I need the

tubers, the fist of them, blunt fat fingers
damned with the furious ting, with the jaggery,
crystals and dust and the bundle of nodules
fermented or dashed in a cake or concoction.
Bring me it, that I might go tooled up,
my last breath searing the eyes of the footman,
splinter and spice in my trinket teeth.

Christina Lindberg: A Collage

from the trailers for *The Depraved, Maid in Sweden*
and *They Call Her One Eye*

When waiting and wanting aren't enough,
you'll see scenes of a girl—young, frightening,
growing up. Previously only whispered about.

She's not a little girl any more. She has
new interests, her own terrible kind of body.
You've seen her in 23 nightmares,

alone on a motion picture screen, everything
there is to know about love. Her nudity
is a weekend you are urged not to attend.

Her speech is unpromotable, a film
of feeling and sexual activity. If you are
embarrassed, put on a new awareness.

Forget revenge and the hard, naked truth.
She has so much to give: mercy, cruelty,
beauty that would make a shambles of you.

In the clutches of her, disaster is experience,
Stockholm a penthouse, the 1970s innocent.
There has never been another coming.

When waiting and wanting aren't enough,
you'll see what was left of every blow,
every cut. Shameful, you'll see all of her.

Josef

I box myself into the kitchen-white Skoda,
scrumping your *Buy milk, eggs, bread* list
in my steadying grip, ashing the kerb
with more scrapings of paint

and leaning the car to the left so it's almost like
a short man bending his knees on a bridge
before jumping. The sun very calmly bakes
my clay flesh into fissured earth,
which means more hand-cream, father—
I shall add that to the scrumped up list.

Why must I suffer Nové Město in the day?
The tram lines cause my head to buffet the car's roof.
I arrive at the store a squared-off bedpost
with arms for hung-up gun holsters.

How I prefer to be a night operator,
clot of shadow, putting out the eye-moon
as I fill up the narrower back-streets,
the stony clank of my strides carrying
all the way to the Vltava and back.
I miss the whispers of the recent dead,
the way the city's outline, close-curtained,
reminds me of a spiked pit.

How I prefer the dusky library
to the sun and its carping tourists,
the sky's fist filled with swifts.

Bullshit-Related Injuries in the A & E

On the gurney, unconscious: man stabbed in the chest with
I'm not racist but. Surgery is on its way. Pulse a bird's blink.

Trauma room, haemorrhage induced by *gave away their human rights*
when they. 'Give me 4 units of O neg, hang two on the rapid infuser.'

The man whose head's been Morris-danced into bandages,
battered repeatedly in the street with *lunacy of the PC brigade.*

That broken striplight's giving everyone a migraine. Same story
in the MIU—minor wounds caused by household affronts to truth:

It's not you, it's me in the eye. Thumb-tip lost to
it's going to be different this time. Tour de force'd while reading.

One of the surgeons discovers the *I'm not a racist but* victim
has also been assaulted with *traditional British values.*

It's Friday. They're bringing in another *just not natural* casualty
'John. John, can you hear me. Airway looks clear.'

'What's her BP?' 'Pulse ox is 82.'
It's not as bad as the day they blew up an *asylum seekers*

are treated better than the rest of us.
Limbs torn clean off. Blood on every pane of glass.

Kuebiko

I've come up his hill's knobbled back.
Wise Kuebiko sees everything from here:
the red kites over the fringes of motorway,
the red kites over the soft skulls of foxgloves,
the teaspoons over the soft skulls of breakfast eggs
the yolky mouths over the remains of breakfast eggs.

Kate and I have come up his hill's clammy back.
Old, wise Kuebiko hears everything from here:
the rill and trill of skylarks at Grimes Graves,
the long, sure breath of flint mines at Grimes Graves,
the long, sure, breath of the coffee machine at regular intervals
the unwrapping of plastic packaging at regular intervals.

Kate and K and I have come up his hill's saurus back.
Bent, old, wise Kuebiko puts up with everything here:
the plague of Cinnabar caterpillars on the burdock,
the plague of joyless coupling in the bedrooms,
the grind of screw-tops opening in the bedrooms,
the grind of steady sunlight in his straw hair.

Kay's 21st

My parents have bought me a single iron handcuff
with P U L S A R bitten into it.
The box it came in reminds me of a child's coffin.
I smile to tell them *This is really great*
and clamp it shut on my wrist.
My mother's smile is a set of rubber kitchen knives.
My father never smiles.

In turn, I unwrap my other presents—
a bullet, my name inscribed on it,
a book comprised entirely of lies,
some kind of killing jar
and so on.
My cake is decorated with marauder ants
who are engaged in a murderous raid on the gentle ants
whose nest is the cake's gooey centre.
Everyone sings *You're shit and you know you are.*

Later, Uncle Alan shakes my hand.
It's hard to shake hands with a warthog.
He asks me about
the silver thread in my eye,
the silver clasp in my heart.
'How do you know when something is really bad?'
I tell him everything is *really* bad
and that being a middle-aged warthog
he ought to appreciate this.

He wipes dead ants from his chin.
I turn back to the scream of window,
the concrete Tesco they built on our garden
and the silverfish wending down the skirting
like goblin mercury.

The Astronomer

I watch. I watch and wonder what it meant.
But nothing I am watching happened less
than centuries ago. The crack of flint
on flint has come to this:

my eye, the cord of glass, the stale light,
the flumes of numbers swallowed by the Mac
and Fireball XL5's enchanted flight
through belt, through gyre, though gas.

The more I watch, the more the sky becomes
a tent pitched by a thousand telescopes,
a giant on all fours, whose dark shift combs
my roof with white-hot pips.

The New Doctor Who

He was sighted in London, 'a great tall blacke man'.
A party of ten were sent out to bring him in,
among them Slaughterford and Jenny Greenteeth.

In Framlingham, word of his wickedness spread.
Three sisters confessed to assisting him.
Learned tracts were published on the Continent.

In April, he passed through Haughley, high
on a police horse. Braziers spat cinder-mouthfuls,
lit the kindling of dawn. A wind bowed.

Poor Black Shuck never came back from the mist.
Balladeers' voices guttered in their throats.
I wrote to John: *A traitor lives among us.*

The Sabbat was held as usual, though many
had hidden or taken the form of rocks
and even the wine had a steely aftertaste.

Some say he wears finely tailored suits
and will sit down to think, chew on livestock.
He laughs when I tell him this. His mouth

is a forge and his laugh is ironmongery.
'How long did you say you were staying?'
'Well now. I don't think I did.'

Henching for Jonathan Crane

I've worn the kit of all the city's worst—
the new-bruise-pink and green of Mr Mirth,
the question-mark motif (I looked a berk
in that one, no mistake)—I've done a turn
in sprigs for Plant-girl (fuck, I fancied her).
You name the crook-cum-freak, I donned the shirt:

King Snake, Black Mask,
Clayface, Mr Zsaz,
Two-Face, Manbat,
Scarface, Ra's al,
Wotsisface, Something-Jack,
Fifth rate bad hats.

Not a one compares to Johnny C,
Führer of Foul Fear, Straw Shah of Screams,
as he'd have had it once, back when his lean-
as-evening-shadows figure was the seat
of something that was still all in one piece
and Scarecrow someone he'd *pretend* to be.

He jerks from vial to flame to flask to book,
moves like those puppets that dance round to tunes.
He keeps birds and doesn't have a costume
as such but wears a stitched-together stew
of rags, a sack mask, bent hat, bits of noose.
We turn up in pretty much what we choose.

When he's configured in his wicker throne,
all knees and nails and elbows as he goes
over the plot's bones, you sense the scope
of his gifts, how every chill you've ever known
that made you piss yourself's stood in a row
right before him, stark as snow on coal.

I guess I'd like to be there when the frost
that keeps him crooked buckles just a jot
and see the frightened boy beneath it, watch
meltwater trickle to and from his gob.
When he recalls his wounds I'll reach across
the field of night and tell him, 'There, there, boss.'

Bedhair

New versions of the tanka of Yosano Akiko

My black bolt of hair
is a mess again—a 'Which Line
Leads Home?' puzzle
where each strand begins, ends
with a different thought of you.

The weekend's a through-train
bulleting past where we stand.
'Not a damn thing lasts,'
I cry, forcing both his hands
to grapple with both my breasts.

Stumbled in, quite wrecked
from an all-nighter. My Guinness-
thick tangled hair
brushes the strings of my Rick.
Only note played since I bought it.

'You've got morning breath,'
I tell him, and slink from his room
one Saturday, pausing
at his strewn, softly crippled jeans,
hoiking them over my hips.

Serious, bird's nest
which-wind-did-I-fuck bedhair.
Just give me a comb
and the morning rain, filtered
through a blackbird's pinions.

He wakes me by crooning
Hallelujah. 'Your hair looks
like a baffled king.'
He chucks me his greasy flick-comb.
I go red and miss the catch.

I was built to wound
men's dark hearts from a distance.
A just punishment:
my blacker than bike-grease hair,
my whiter than salt-flake skin.

1910

Egon is 'wolf-handsome', 'young', 'a talent'.
Everything he's done tonight was bought
with borrowed crowns—*Burgtheater*, billiards, restaurant.
He's broke now but surviving on a current
of affluence. He is no *sansculotte*;
his manner is too grim, his clothes too decent.

Those skinny things he lures in from the street
fixate upon the steep expanse of brow
and beneath it, all his features in a knot,
while his hand, on its lunge, reels wildly about.
He seems designed to intimately thaw,
then braise like so much meat the homeless heart.

Who, then, is this contortionist who's packed
his shoulders in, drawn up his hips' ridge and climbed
into the canvas, this shock of half-stick-insect?
Whose bones are these, remote and derelict?
Who is this wastrel, hook-spined, puppet-limbed,
this goblin who ogles a girl's near-naked act?

Could be they were him but he, hating them,
cut everywhere their bodies joined to his
and banged them up in his sanitorium,
these sheets being windows into each white room,
and each day does his rounds, surveys each face
to make sure all that's left in him is him.

Could be all he sees each morning, shaving,
is Egon—up-and-comer, friend of Klimt—
and, traumatised by, ultimately, nothing
perfects the mirrors that will hang like dinner gongs,
ringing with the proofs of inner torment,
and lets them enter him, scantling by scantling.

Boy

I was the Valiant Soldier and so were you.
We took it in turns to be the one slew Boy,
now recalling the teeth that were butcher hooks,

now the pike that was glazed with silver and salt,
the massive, heart-swallowing mouth of Boy,
the tempest of minion and falconet.

Publicans, stable boys, nobles and nobles' wives—
all of them craned for the tale of the killing of Boy.
No one guessed, or if they did, didn't say

that we'd not even sniffed a burning cord of matchlock
and only heard of the dense, cream curls of Boy,
so we won the flesh that seared us more than grapeshot.

Do you feel it too? Throughout the world,
the night is hot and hot with the breath of Boy.
My woman is cold and the punks are especially cold.

Severed by blood, the weapon-proof witches' ally,
Boy, his wounds still running. The gun-dog Boy,
who did catch bullets and spat them, frothing with acid.

I could cross the sea but I could not outrun Boy.
Nuzzling my ribs, his head a bull's head, is Boy,
and when I sleep I sleep in the snarl of Boy.

Legendary

This is the pub where Perkin Warbeck fought.
That blot you've stood your pint in there's his bloodstain.
Upstairs, countless plotters would consort.
The jukebox might as well be Nick Drake's headstone
and Will Kemp danced from here to Diss one Whitsun,
starting with a jar. This scuffed banquette
was graced in '83 by Solzhenitsyn,
who'd stopped off on his way to . . . I forget.
The bust Lee-Enfield was H Rider Haggard's.
Above the bar—see? Pankhurst propped her placards
over by the dartboard, all handwritten!
And this is where my marriage hit the jaggeds.
In fact, this is *The Guinness Book of Record*'s
third most woebegotten pub in Britain.

(The Dark Lord Must Be) Aubade

I wake at four and find I'm still half-drunk.
The light's already edged the bedroom blind
but misses flanks and ankles that are sunk
in other flanks where bodies lie entwined.
I mourn the dying of the soundless dark
that stamped our ritual like a watermark
and dread the day to come, the being clean,
the suit and tie that grip me in their vice
(the boring kind of 'vice'),
the daily dosage of fluoxetine.

No teasing sexual act is half as hard
to bear as what the light will now carve out:
the crackless Ouroboros of façade
to which we're each unshakably devout.
As ultimate as death, as desolate,
but full of promise and more cruel for it.
Small wonder we few make our brief escape
into trance-like states through all these rites—
these wild, nebulous nights—
and try to take on more unearthly shape.

It's not as if that world we usher in
with drums and nakedness beneath the moon
is any more fantastic than the one
that's dreamt of in the blunt light of the sun.
Its adherents all talk and act as if
it's real and therefore act it into life.
We do the same—the only difference is
that they outnumber us and most of us

are also them because
we have to be. That's my analysis.

The bowls of unused condoms on the floor
I gather up and empty. I take fresh
towels out of the airing cupboard for
my guests and leave them by the bluff of flesh.
I programme the hot water to stay on
another hour or so. I find the stone
the Priestess smothered in her rubious breast
while taking every partner in her stride.
I toss it back outside
and only then half-heartedly get dressed.

Voronoff's Patient

Look, my face is full again, my jaw
a stirrup for a newly-soled tongue.
And that's me on the cover of the BMJ

in boxer briefs, curling weights.
Love, I'm remade from the groin out,
begun with a backwards robbery.

As if it were a curse, not a cure,
an offering to horn-crowned Baphomet,
the surgeon sewed into my scrotal purse

a quartered chimp-bollock, one which
I'd earlier watched him sever, his hand
doubtless steadied by destiny's mooring line.

I half-hear the stories of blasphemy,
beasts packed in crates, farmed, the demand,
the outrage at each bone church blackened,

those who ask how much of me is monkey.
Well? Do I bare my plush gums, stretch
my sweetly muscled arms to tear

at a boy's taut cheek? Do I howl
or do I make you howl instead? Babble
that froths in a back room harmlessly.

I picture myself, teeth replenished
with polished chips of garnet, quartz,
leading my grandsons, three wars from now,

horse-skin grafted where shrapnel bit,
and my chopped talisman, still juiced,
still going like the perfect pendulum.

Malignants

People were enthralled by witches, prodigies and omens because,
in an age of catastrophe, they feared for their futures.
    Malcolm Gaskill, *Witchfinders*

By the 1970s they no longer flew bareback on goats,
their nakedness dark against the moon.
And you would not find them clustered
in clearings heady with unguent,
thundering their heels on felled crosses.

Instead they ran rental shops,
wove the black tape round toothy spools,
chanting canticles to ward off magnetism.
Orgiastic dances were out; Cannibal Holocaust was in.
Shelf-space once afforded to grimoires,
scrying dishes and sigillated candle-holders
was given up to contraband copies of *The Evil Dead,*
Driller Killer and *I Spit on Your Grave.*

Now they are among those who file-share.
Using GoogleEarth, they plan with precision
the path of the plague, where to best hit the harvest.
I've seen the photographs of missing children
hand in hand with the tall and pear-calved lady,
the ligature of her chignon, her steep sunglasses.
I've heard how they come to be so far abroad:
zapped there as clouds of atoms
by a headless bear-spirit.

The pond in Gerrards Cross has turned to blood
and the Gallagher brothers dip their shirts in it.
The perennial glow at night is said to be
a build-up of radiation from thousands of hexings.
I myself saw the Shee-Cavaliers last week,
careening in front of cars. I caught one's eye
and it was gemmed a raw scarlet.

But I hear that juries are acquitting them.
I hear that gifts of cursed eggs are exchanged
and that witnesses grow the tails of oxen.
Thank God, I say, for *A Magazine of Scandall,*
for *The True Informer* and organs like them.

Oh, yesterday, a child of 12 fathered an imp,
and yet the government are worse than useless.

They Never See Themselves

after Nathaniel Hawthorne's Feathertop

The first confessor is the shop window of Boots, Fleet Street. You think you see a lone stick of straw nosing out of your collar. Your hand goes to your neck, plucks out the culprit, and you give it to the scatter of wind as a bus bellows past.

Piece by piece, your reflections give you up. In the Gents', fat raindrops of mice spill from your sleeve and slalom the sink. Your eyes, whilst shaving, are revealed as last year's acorns, the Bic razor scuffing and blunting on mud-brown hessian—worn smooth where you were frequently kissed.

On the night of your tryst with the boss's daughter, you stand naked in front of a full-length mirror, working your fingers through your chest's tied-tight bail, removing, one after another, butchered pieces of Massey Ferguson—an eighth of a tyre that was your diaphragm, a wiry nest of alveoli, a chimney stack that served as some bone.

You feel yourself getting lighter, lesser, until Polly, woken by the thudding of parts on her Saxony, flings her arms around you. You want to tell her *I'm not a real man. I'm held together by an enchanted suit.* But you know she'd just say *Save the excuses for later* or *There's no such thing as a 'real man'* and she can never see what you see in all this glass.

Spell For Those Whose Hair Causes Them Anxiety

You may have been caught in the wake of a curse
as it luffed up into the just-turned night
or come fresh from advents more diabolic
still. Now you quarrel with furrow and forelock,
uncultured kiss-curls and crown, and you fight
and wrench at it, aiming for casual muss.

Throw out your trophy case—half-full gourds
stood in the cabinet you gaze into
while you carve up your scalp with a comb.
Fill it with candles, wizard's teeth, chrome
'til it's jammed and wait for the portamento
of wind to storm in with its cubs and chords.

Against Free Speech

No stutter for me—instead, what leaves
listeners hanging by their china cup handles,
crowded at the pieshop window of my breath,
itching to plug in their own cunning tongues

are the long pauses when I find that
I've overshot something, and I remember that
the words must come from somewhere
and the chanting in my head grows louder.

I never knew my godfather's mother,
who could finish your sentences two, three,
four leaps of logic from the end. Perhaps
she would always surprise you by saying

not what you were going to say
and not what you meant to say
but what the saying itself thought
it should make for, its heart's nodding lantern.

Imagine if every thought that never made it
to your lips came stumbling from your mouth
right now—the ruin beyond all repair,
the sense of betrayal strong as a noose.